let's move
sports movement patterns

Thank you to Coaches Karen and Dean for believing in this,

and to my editor, Connie Berg.

Thank you to Charles Figallo OSJ OAM.

To the original SMAC team members David, John and Jess.

A special thanks to Coach Kimberlee,

the MFT (Master Functional Trainers) family,

my Mum and Dad, and Tanisha and Lachlan.

Let's Move: Sports Movement Patterns by John Connelly
ISBN 978-0-6481963-0-3
Copyright © 2017 John Connelly. All rights reserved.
Design and illustration by Dean Lahn
Editing by Connie M. Berg
First Published in Australia 2017 by SMAC

www.movingwell.org
coach.john@movingwell.org

let's move

sports movement patterns

by John Connelly

Introduction

Let's move anywhere, anytime and with anyone.

Hi, this is Coach John.

It's my aim to assist young people to get the best out of the sports they play by mastering the Sports Movement Patterns.

In this book, I'd like to introduce you to Coach Karen and her team, who will share with us the importance and relevance of each Movement Pattern.

Both of us know that every child is different, and have found that combining the Sports Movement Patterns assists children to become better at the sports they play.

Solid foundations can be achieved by combining the Sports Movement Patterns in this series with regular training that's engaging, that has lots of variety, and most importantly is FUN.

In the following pages we will learn from Coach Karen and her team the following ten Sports Movement Patterns

- Run (gait)
- Upper body twist
- Pull
- Push
- Hinge
- Lunge
- Squat
- Jump
- Lower body twist
- Kick

Let's go meet Coach Karen and her new team as they introduce themselves to you, the sports they play and the Sports Movement Pattern they use.

Let's get moving!

It's our first day together, and I am very excited to coach the team.

Okay team! As it's our first day together, please introduce yourself and share with me what sports you play, with who, and where?

I'll start first.

I compete in triathlons and train with my partner at the local pool, park and city.

I feel excited when I finish a race.

Come along and let's meet everyone.

Rugby

I play with my friends.
We run around a lot.

I've gotten really fast at running,
and I scored a try for my team!

My team mates made
me feel like a winner!

That is fantastic.
Thanks for sharing, Charlie.
Well done!

Netball

I play a catch and pass game with my sisters.

twist

I have to twist to get the ball past them. We try to be faster than each other.

My dad cheers when I get a pass off, and I feel a little embarrassed but happy!

That is excellent. Thanks for sharing, Niree. Well done!

Cricket

It's my game and I play it with my uncles.

pull

We play at the oval. They help me to learn to catch the ball, pulling the ball into my chest when it's been hit very high.

My uncles have helped me to be less afraid of the ball. I caught a player out, and the cheers from my team were fantastic!

smac

That is fabulous.
Thanks for sharing, Tommi.
Well done!

Soccer

It's our family game and we play it in my Nanna's back yard.

Whenever the ball goes out of bounds, I get to throw it in as far as I can. It's a big overhead push is how Nanna taught me.

When the ball went out during the game, I threw the ball to our best player, and she was able to score.

The team and I were cheering!

That is spectacular. Thanks for sharing, Gina. Well done!

Volleyball

It's my favourite time 'cause I get to go to the beach to play with my mum and older sister, Tiffany.

Tiffany helps me to dig in and return the ball—it's called the hinge, and it's one of the basic movements of volleyball.

Wow! On game day I returned many serves and Tiffany was amazed. I feel I can do so much more now.

That is magnificent.
Thanks for sharing, Suresh.
Well done!

Hockey

Gemma, Maddison and I play together. Gemma and Maddison are my cousins.

lunge

We play block and pass which helps me to practice my lunge while blocking. Gemma is really good at blocking, and Maddison at passing.

With their help, I was able to defend our goals from many of the other team's shots. My cousins were surprised how well I did and I can't wait to play again!

That is outstanding. Thanks for sharing, Nicole. Well done!

Softball

When I stay on the farm, I get to play with my auntie and her friends.

squat

I play catcher, so I squat a lot, but with my asthma I don't have to run as much. I still get to join in and have fun.

I feel accepted and a part of the team.

That is dynamite.
Thanks for sharing, Abby.
Well done!

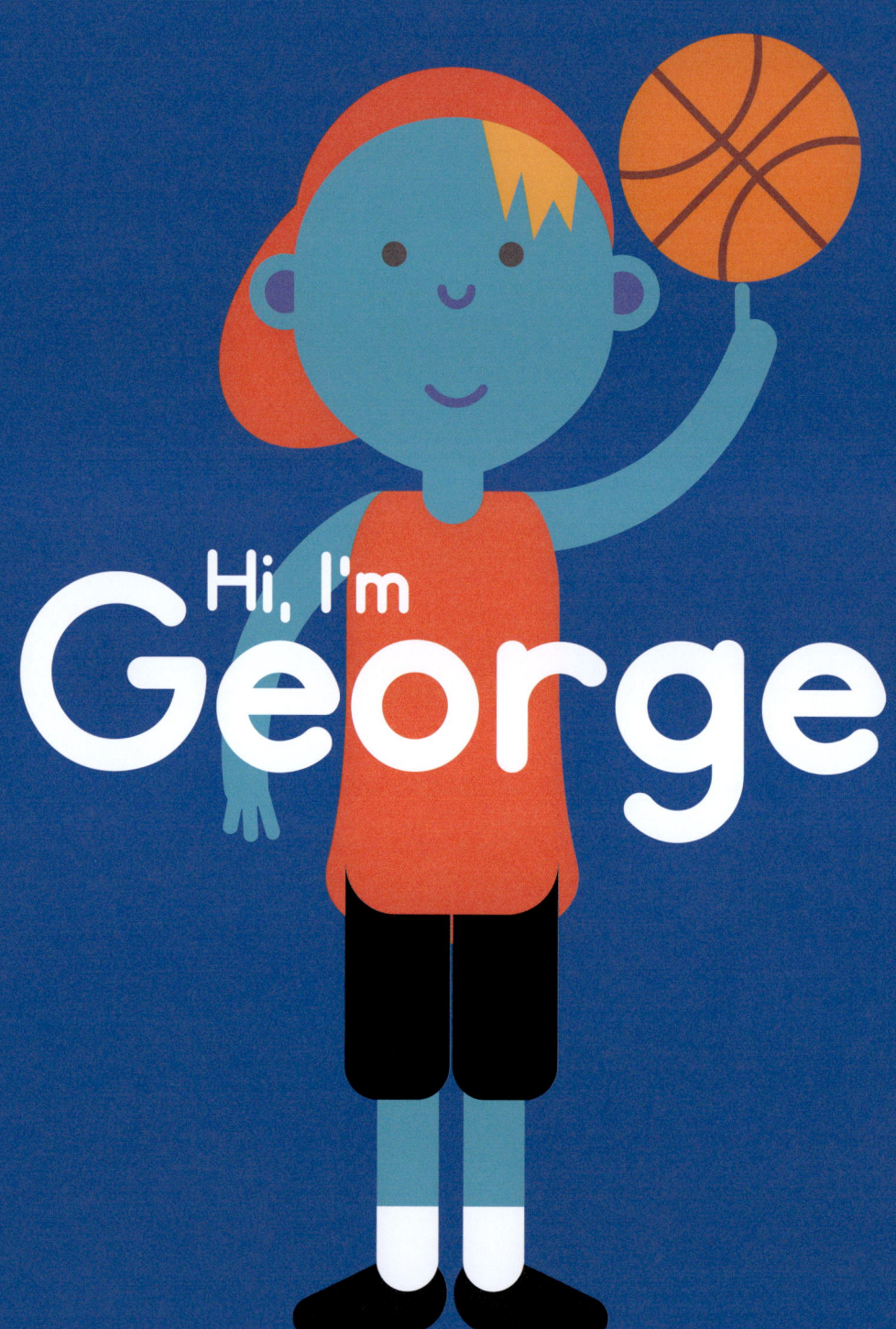

Basketball

It's the best, my Grandpa still plays too!

My Grandpa is tall so I have to jump really high to get the ball off him! We go to the courts by my house where other kids and parents join in.

I'm happy when I get to play and show off what I have learnt from Grandpa.

That is incredible. Thanks for sharing, George. Well done!

Ten Pin Bowling

I play with my friends at the local bowling centre.

We do some lower body twists before bowling so we are ready to go. We're getting good enough we can bowl without bumpers.

lower body twist

I got my first strike without bumpers in front of everyone! My team gave me a big hug to celebrate.

That is beautiful. Thanks for sharing, Peta. Well done!

Footy

Aussie Rules! It's my favourite game. I love to play with my brother and sister.

We try to not let the ball touch the ground to see how many kicks and passes we can do to each other.

kick

When my coach says I've gotten better, I'm really proud.

smac

That is awesome. Thanks for sharing, Travis. Well done!

Good to meet you!
Join our team! Introduce yourself:

Hi, I'm ....
....

I like to play ....
....

with ....
....

Draw yourself playing your favourite sport.

This sure was fun, Coach John!

Thank you, Coach Karen, for the opportunity to meet your team.

Let's thank the team for helping us learn about:

- Charlie–Running
- Niree–Upper body twist
- Tommi–Pull
- Gina–Push
- Suresh–Hinge
- Nicole–Lunge
- Abby–Squat
- George–Jump
- Peta–Lower body twist
- Travis–Kick

By combining the Sports Movement Patterns in this series with your regular training, young people will develop the foundations for playing sports and moving well.

Follow the *Let's Move* series of books to learn more, and remember these are used

anywhere, anytime, and with anyone!

Printed by Libri Plureos GmbH in Hamburg, Germany